Copyright © 2021

C000124526

Contacts

— Email: service@thehackerish.com

— Twitter: @thehackerish

Cover photo by Анна Рыжкова from Pexels

Foreword

The bug bounty hunting community is full of technical resources. However, any successful hunter will tell you that succeeding takes more than technical knowledge.

Without the proper mindset, the effective tactics, and some vital soft skills, here is the hard truth: You won't last in the bug bounty hunting game. You might submit a few reports at first, but you won't stand the lack of motivation when you can't find bugs for a few weeks. Worst yet, you will lose your self-esteem when almost all of your reports won't be accepted. After months, the situation may even develop into burnout.

If you understand and exploit known security vulnerabilities in CTF challenges but still struggle to find bugs in real-world targets, this book is for you. However, if you have no clue what a SQL injection is, I recommend starting with a training[1] first.

I wrote this book with a single purpose in mind: Help you understand and master the essential skills to

---

[1] https://subscribepage.com/owasp_top_ten_hands_on_training_lab

become a successful bug bounty hunter. At the same time, I want it to be entertaining.

To achieve this goal, I designed the book around the story of Anna, a fictitious Junior Security Engineer who has just heard of bug bounty hunting. Throughout her fascinating journey, you will discover all the steps she took, from start to finish.

You will witness how she took her first steps to acquire the necessary knowledge, observe all the limits she discovers about herself, and grasp all the proven solutions she came up with to overcome them.

In six months, she will collect 1000 reputation points on HackerOne, get invited to hack on private programs, and earn her first $5000 along the way.

Whether you have just started or have spent years in this industry, you will undoubtedly identify with the different hurdles throughout the story. I am sure you will add some missing tricks to your toolset to succeed in bug bounty hunting.

For the technical aspect of the story, you will find appendices that support Anna's journey. There, you will discover how to approach a bug bounty program for the first time and how to perform in-depth web application hacking to increase your chances of finding bugs.

You can read this book cover to cover while bookmarking the pivot points. Then, go back to each crucial moment whenever you face the same situation.

Sit tight and enjoy the ride!

Table of content

A bug bounty hunting journey

journey

Overcome your limits and become a successful hunter

Too good to be true

"Don't make friends who are comfortable to be with. Make friends who will force you to lever yourself up." — Thomas J. Watson

I remember that meeting as if it were yesterday. It is nearly sunset. I'm sitting with my friend around a coffee after work. The spacious, relatively calm terrace hosts few clients. I feel the fresh breeze on my skin.

— "I am planning to buy the course and become an Offensive Security Certified Professional[2]. Do you think it is a good idea?" I ask.

— "That's an ambitious step forward! Do you have what it takes?" She replies.

I pause for a moment, take a sip of the freshly brewed hot coffee. Then reply.

— "I think so; I know basic networking, and I have been practicing web application hacking for about six months. I feel ready. What do you think?".

— "OSCP is a prestigious certification; I highly encourage you to take it. But I am afraid you will find it challenging with the current experience you have."

My friend Julia got into computer hacking earlier than I. She holds many infosec certifications, OSCP included. We met each other at university. She had

---

[2] https://thehackerish.com/oscp-certification-all-you-need-to-know

given hacking training for the cybersecurity club members back then. Naturally, her opinion was important to me.

Recently, I have been hesitating to apply, but I have to trust myself if I want to advance my career in the Information Security industry.

Julia's answer, however, has just made me nervous. I am starting to doubt my capabilities. Is OSCP that hard? How challenging can it get? From the different reviews I read about it, I agree it is not for the faint of heart. Maybe I need to practice in another way?

I am distracted for a while, but my line of thoughts gets interrupted when Julia smiles for a moment.

— "How many machines have you rooted?" she asks.

— "Few on Root-me." I reply.

Root-me.org is a website Julia gave me months ago. It contains diversified security challenges from many different categories. The platform hosts machines that anyone can spin up and hack online to become root, the most privileged user on a Linux system.

— She replies with a smile on her face, "Then I guess you aren't ready...yet".

Her sarcastic smile made me feel uncomfortable, but I appreciate her honesty. OSCP's practice lab and hands-on exam both contain machines I must root, and I can say for sure that is not an area I have practiced well.

— "There are plenty of machines on an emerging platform called hackthebox.eu", she adds.

I grab my phone from my pocket and take note of this website; I can't wait to see what it has to offer! I will surely give it a try as soon as I arrive home.

— "I am assuming you will pay for OSCP from your pocket." she says.

— "Indeed, I have no income stream other than my full-time job salary."

— "What if I told you that you could learn and practice more computer hacking while earning money? Would you be willing to do it?"

For me, the idea of a side hustle job is something I had tried before. I had signed up on a freelance website and translated some articles for a client because I know three languages. I also like graphic design; I had uploaded some of my creations to a print-on-demand service to earn a commission whenever someone uses my art. However, I didn't enjoy it much. The competition is becoming more challenging, and I had to find a competitive advantage, which means that I had to be serious if I wanted to succeed. I thought I would earn easy money doing such trivial freelancing jobs, but I was wrong! My expectations were seemingly too high, and I lacked the motivation to keep translating documents or creating graphic designs. After all, I already have a salary to pay my bills, and I am not in urgent need of money, at least at the moment.

— "I don't feel I have enough expertise to offer penetration testing services as a freelancer. Customers will choose established candidates with a proven professional experience". I reply.

— "That's true unless you don't need to be a professional to get started." She replies confidently.

— "What do you mean? I am not sure I get your point".

— "You can choose which clients you want to hack, and you get paid for each vulnerability that you find. You don't have to wait until some client selects you."

You are kidding me! This is too good to be true. If I

heard this claim from a random person, I would walk away without hesitation.

— "Then how the client would trust you will do a professional job?". I ask skeptically.

— "Clients don't have to trust you; they trust the system. There is currently a crowd of hackers poking around all kinds of public assets on the internet. I bet most of them don't know what they are doing, some of them find vulnerabilities here and there, but few are the elite who find loads of bugs in most of the targets they test".

She pauses for a moment to take a sip. Then she says: "It is called bug bounty hunting."

I have never heard of that term before! I know a bounty hunter is someone who pursues criminals and captures them in exchange for a reward.

— "Much like Django Unchained, the movie?" I ask.

— "Oh, you've seen it too. Yeah, that's the same thing. You are the cowboy in the wild west web. Instead of criminals, you hunt for security bugs".

This is getting fun! I picture myself riding the network traffic on the wild internet, looking here and there for security bugs, and getting paid along the way. The beauty of it is that I don't need to compete with other bounty hunters like in the typical freelancing gigs. I am independent; I work when and how it pleases me.

— "But wait, how am I supposed to find what targets I have the right to hack?" I suddenly ask.

— "Ah! Good question. These are called bug bounty programs. There are some well-established ones. Google, Facebook, Microsoft all have their own. But it's generally not that easy to find bugs there. Instead, you can choose from a large pool of targets on bug bounty platforms. Some hunters hack on all of them, and others are loyal to only one. It depends on your taste and where you feel comfortable. Did I mention that you can sign up and start hacking right now?"

This all seems too good to be true! All the alarms are firing in my head, yet my defense levels are surprisingly low because I hear it from a friend I trust.

This concept is new to me, and I certainly need to explore it further. Plus, it could be a good opportunity for me to prepare for the OSCP while earning money.

Later, I knew I was wrong.

Why is the start always hard?

"A journey of a thousand miles begins with a single step." — Lao Tzu

On my way home, I google "bug bounty hunting" on my phone. Sure enough, I find what seems to be some bug bounty platforms. I create an account on HackerOne[3] and Bugcrowd[4] and see what targets they offer.

To my surprise, there are plenty to choose from, just like Julia said to me. I recognize Yahoo! and Twitter among the results, but I don't think it's a good idea to hack them with my current expertise.

The next day, I get up earlier. What a beautiful sunny morning! I prepare some coffee and go straight to the couch. I open my laptop and sign in to Bugcrowd.

I am trying to find what I should hack. Because I want to earn money, I filter only the paying programs. I notice Tesla from the results, and I jump right in.

I think I am going to start with the main website. I hesitate for a moment; I have never tested a real website before. Nevertheless, I have to jump out of my comfort zone. I tell myself: "Just make the first

---

[3] www.hackerone.com

[4] www.bugcrowd.com

step".

I visit the website on Firefox, browse every page, and click on every link. The more I dig into the website, the more confused I get. All the links have the same structure, which is the friendly name of the page title. I can't find any page that stands out and no promising parameters that I can attack!

Half an hour later, all I have is a massive number of useless pages and an angry computer that has spun its loud fans to keep up with the load of work. Is this how I am supposed to hunt for bugs?

I stand up while scratching my head, trying to come up with an answer. So far, I learned basic vulnerabilities and practiced my knowledge on mini-challenges dedicated to teaching one weakness at a time. However, Tesla's website is much more significant. Besides, I'm used to hacking websites that already contain vulnerabilities. Therefore, I usually focus on how to exploit them. Today, I'm not sure if this website is even vulnerable! Since I don't know what to look for, how on earth am I supposed to hack this website? Maybe bug bounty hunting isn't as easy as I thought it would be. If I want to find bugs, I need to learn more about how others do it.

I spend a few hours looking on the internet for resources on bug bounty hunting techniques. I stumble upon the Web Application Hacker's Handbook[5], the second edition. A glance at the summary reveals to me how serious this book is. It seems to be covering a great deal of web application hacking and has a significant number of positive reviews. I think it is going to be a good investment for me down the road. So, I order it.

While waiting for the book to arrive, I watch some YouTube videos from various bug bounty hunters talking about their methodologies. I enjoyed the talk "How to shot web"[6] by Jason Haddix, which explains a process that follows a set of structured steps. I recognize most of them from what I have learned about penetration testing, but the tools are new. Besides, the approach seems reliable and exhaustive, but I feel it is overkill for a beginner like me.

Then, I watch all the YouTube playlist videos "Web Hacking Pro Tips"[7] by Peter Yaworski, where he

---

[5] https://thehackerish.com/the-best-hacking-books-for-ethical-hackers/#wahh

[6] https://www.youtube.com/watch?v=-FAjxUOKbdI

[7] https://www.youtube.com/watch?v=2R4YXEAG6AI

interviews a handful of bug bounty hunters. He asks many questions, such as how they started in hacking, how they approach a target, what they do for a living, and many more. Some concepts seem a bit tricky for me. I might come back later If I need to.

Since most of the community is present on Twitter, I search for "bug bounty" and subscribe to most of the accounts from the results. Shortly after, my Twitter feed is full of security-related content, with a significant portion on bug bounty hunting.

To get a feel of what issues other bug bounty hunters find, I also read as many reports as I can from HackerOne's Hacktivity[8], which lists publicly disclosed bug bounty reports found by hackers on the platform.

These resources opened my eyes! Indeed, bug bounty hunting requires more work than I expected. It seems so apparent how ignorant I am and how much I still have to learn.

Once I receive the book, I start devouring it right away. It is enormous, but it answers so many questions I had in mind; How to approach a real

---

[8] https://hackerone.com/hacktivity

website? How to look for vulnerabilities? And many more.

I keep reading until I reach the application mapping chapter. I learn how to use a web proxy to discover web applications.

I hop on the couch, open my computer, and then launch Burp Suite Community Edition[9], a free web proxy mostly used by bug bounty hunters and penetration testers. I start browsing Tesla's website the same way as before. Only this time, I am proxying the traffic through Burp Suite. After a brief tour around the website, I launch the spider. I eagerly wait for any exciting results, such as weird pages, endpoints, or parameters. A few minutes later, I get nothing! I only hear the fans' noise and feel the heat of my laptop on my legs.

Again, not the ideal approach for such a flagship website with my limited 4GB of RAM and Core 2 Duo CPU. I have to be more effective without overwhelming neither my computer nor Tesla's website.

I notice some new subdomains in the spider results.

---

[9] https://portswigger.net/burp/communitydownload

Maybe I should start with one of those subdomains. I might get lucky and find an overlooked bug.

I'm staring at the screen to locate any curious name from the subdomains list when I hear my phone alarm ringing. It's time to go to bed.

My first bug bounty

"I find that the harder I work, the more luck I seem to have."
— Thomas Jefferson

I got distracted by work recently. I haven't hacked for days. But I make sure to read at least a few pages of the book I purchased. Every chapter opens my eyes to new knowledge.

And then it hits me! I was approaching the target from the wrong angle. Instead of desperately looking for those low-hanging fruits, such as backup files, or outstanding parameters that I am used to finding in CTF[10] websites, I should take a step back and look at the website from a bigger perspective.

The book talks about enumerating features. Instead, I was listing pages! I can see how distracted I was, desperately looking for individual pages without any context, trying to find a weakness without understanding how the target works.

It makes sense to focus on each feature at a time, which would help me get the big picture, categorize the endpoints, and analyze the flow one step at a time.

The next weekend, I log into my HackerOne account and pick a bug bounty program. I don't want to go back to Tesla; I want to start fresh. Any online

---

[10] Capture the flag

solution with a considerable number of features would do the job. I also want to try the HackerOne platform.

While searching in the directory, I find a design company that offers an online tool that intuitively helps designers create prototypes.

This time, instead of blindly spidering the entire website, I create an account and try to enumerate and understand as many features as I can. To do that, I simply use it like any regular user would, while taking mental notes.

Authentication is the first feature I notice. I remember that the book I am reading has an entire chapter on that. A user can then create a project, define a canvas, and design a prototype based on predefined visual elements. As I am interacting with the application, I am looking at the generated requests in Burp Suite.

Whenever I click on a button or drag an element to the canvas, I see simultaneous calls to both static and dynamic endpoints. The former fetch static content such as JavaScript, CSS, fonts, and image files, while the latter reveals lengthy endpoints with many parameters. I feel intimidated by the vast amount of data my mind needs to process and understand. Plus, those static files irritate me. There has to be a way to get rid of them! I tinker with Burp Suite's interface and find that I can hide files by extension using the filter feature, great! Now, I can focus on only the relevant things.

After a few hours, my mind starts picking up patterns, and I gradually become familiar with the features, the URL structures, and the parameter names. Now I feel comfortable focusing on one functionality.

I choose the project creation feature because it is the first step a user would naturally do in the nominal flow. Plus, it is intuitive. So, I create a new project and look at the HTTP calls in my web proxy. There is a POST request which uses an anti-CSRF token. However, I notice that the application uses the same value when I create another project. This behavior doesn't align with what I learned about mitigations for CSRF[11]. The anti-CSRF should be unique per request. My heart starts beating as I'm staring at the screen. It might be my first vulnerability!

I try to think about the impact of this behavior for a while. A user can automate the creation of projects to

---

[11] https://cheatsheetseries.owasp.org/cheatsheets/Cross-Site_Request_Forgery_Prevention_Cheat_Sheet.html

spam the team, but I am not convinced. Meanwhile, a part of my mind just wants to file a report on HackerOne. I can feel my heart beating as I furiously start typing on the keyboard. I make sure to explain how a static anti-CSRF token is not a good practice. After about 10 minutes, I hit the submit button. My report is now in the "open" state, waiting for the team to pick it up.

It's time to take a break.

The next Monday, I'm in my office doing some task when I receive a notification from HackerOne; it seems that one of the program members commented on my report. Indeed, they recognize that the anti-CSRF token should be unique per request. However, due to performance issues and the minimal security impact, they are not considering a fix. Therefore, my report is closed as Informative, which means they won't fix it.

I can reply to the comment and ask for a revision. But before that, I want to revise my knowledge. I quickly open Firefox and visit the OWASP documentation about CSRF. I start reading anxiously.

In the first paragraphs, there is nothing new to me. Cross-Site Request Forgery is a vulnerability that occurs when the application allows state-changing operations, such as creating a project in my case, without validating the requester on the server. Therefore, I can prepare a simple form and host it online. When the victim opens my page, the web browser initiates a project creation request, along with her session cookie.

As a solution, the server usually sends a hidden random token along with the form, then verifies if it is the same when the user sends the state-changing request.

I focus on the mitigation section and notice that the OWASP recommends either a unique token per page or per session. Damn! What I reported is not a vulnerability since the program uses the second recommendation.

It doesn't make sense to reply anymore; I am already grateful they closed my report as informative. There is worse, the NA status!

Shortly after, I receive another notification from HackerOne. When I open it, I can't believe my eyes! I can hear my heartbeat getting faster as I realize that the program was kind enough to honor my effort with $150!

I can't believe it happened! I scored my first bug! Well, not a real one, but my report got closed as valid. I feel an urge to get off my chair and start dancing. If I were alone in the office, I would have done it for sure.

It's extraordinary how such an act of generosity can give a massive push of confidence to someone barely starting in bug bounty hunting, enough to make me stick to it. For that, I am grateful.

However, I am sure it only happens once. Not all programs would give free money. I need to find real bugs that I can be proud of.

Since this is my first payout, HackerOne asks me to fill up a tax form, which I do. The process is smooth as butter; all I have to do is click on a link they provide that redirects me to the online form. After I e-sign it, I can accept payments.

The next day, I receive the reward via PayPal.

I think I will focus on HackerOne; I loved the overall experience, from signing up to receiving my first bounty. Plus, I prefer to focus on building my reputation on one platform. Maybe I can hack on other platforms in the future.

Although rewarding, the bounty is not the source of my entire excitement. In fact, I proved that bug bounty is not a scam but a model that works. Even though what I found is not a bug, the reward gave me the assurance and the motivation to stick to bug bounty hunting and earn money.

N/A, Informative, and Reputation

"We should not give up, and we should not allow the problem to defeat us." — a. P. J. Abdul kalam

My first bounty gave me a huge motivation that pushed me forward. In my free time, if I am not reading the Web Application Hacker's Handbook, I am applying my knowledge on bug bounty programs. The start is always hard, but I enjoy it so far.

On one program, I am testing the authentication flow when I notice that there is an oracle. In other words, I get different messages depending on the existence of the username. Therefore, I can enumerate valid account names. However, the application locks a user out when a login brute-force is detected. Consequently, I can lock arbitrary users out.

This issue seems legit to me. After all, the security risk is more apparent and convincing than my previous one. So, I write the report explaining in detail what's wrong with this account lockout logic. I first start with a summary where I explain which feature and how it is vulnerable. Then, I develop my idea in the description section. Then comes the impact section, explaining that arbitrary users could be locked out in a massive attack. Finally, I suggest they get rid of the information leak that allows username enumeration in the first place. A generic error would be enough.

After two weeks, my report gets closed as informative.

Reading the developer's reply, I learn that they have a process that detects and stops massive account lockout. At the end of his answer, the developer politely asks me to reopen my report if I disagree.

I resist the urge to reply and think for a moment. Obviously, I can't verify if there is any massive lockout. I would have to target either real accounts or create enough dummy test accounts. The former approach is unethical, and the second is tiresome. Instead of engaging in a conversation that will cost me time and effort with no guarantee that somebody might accept my report, I prefer to invest it by looking for additional bugs.

I file several reports here and there, but almost all of them are closed as Informative. I feel hopeless and frustrated. What am I doing wrong?

I pick a new bug bounty program to have a fresh start again. I find it hard to stick to a bug bounty program once I send them a report. At the same time, I always have to spend a few hours trying to understand how the new application works.

Here I am on this new web application, enumerating its features in the hope of finding a bug. After spending some hours going through almost all of them, I notice that the application sends an SMS to the authenticated user. Looking closely at the HTTP request, I see the phone number in the POST data. When I change it, I surprisingly get an SMS on my other phone!

Unfortunately, I cannot edit the SMS's content, so all I can do is spam arbitrary phone numbers with unsolicited SMS messages. I run the same request through Burp Suite's Intruder to test if I can send many. To my surprise, I could send around 500 SMS messages to my other phone.

I think there is hope for this issue to be accepted. If spamming is not a security risk for the business, consuming the SMS credit is. So, I craft a report using the same structure as before. This time, I explain that they should implement rate-limiting to stop SMS-bombing attacks.

The next day, I receive a shocking notification. Someone from the HackerOne Triage team has closed my report as NA! Which is short for Not Applicable. I rapidly scan the reply to spot any valid reason. Sure enough, I come to know that my finding is out of scope. I nervously visit the bug bounty program's policy to double-check. Indeed, SMS-bombing is there, verbatim!

I quickly go to my HackerOne profile to list my reputation history, and I notice that it has dropped by five points. I also see that my Signal has fallen to around zero because of my recent informative submissions, indicating a considerable noise in my reports. That's not good at all!

The Signal is a float number between -10 and 7. The highest value means there is no noise because all the submissions are valid. I need to get this value close to seven.

Focusing on improving my Signal will automatically improve my reputation. To achieve this, I have to avoid sending Not Applicable or informative reports. But how am I going to do that? I can prevent Not Applicable submissions by thoroughly reading the program's policy and ensuring not to test either known or out of scope issues. But what about informative reports?

I look through my informative submissions to notice a similar pattern. Almost all of them contain debatable issues; they don't have a clear impact.

If I want to reduce informative reports, I have to resist

the urge to report debatable issues. It is tempting to file a new report whenever I find a weird behavior, but my experience so far tells me that's a bad idea. If I want to reduce my noise and increase my reputation, I have to dig deeper and report only the undeniable issues with an impact that no one can deny.

Digging deeper requires me to focus on a single web application, therefore one bug bounty program. So far, I have been hopping from one program to another, hoping to find low-hanging fruits. But since I am dealing with old bug bounty programs, the chance is slim. I might get lucky hitting a freshly updated feature, but I am not willing to take the risk anymore.

Few weeks go by, and I can only say that my new strategy has proved to be working. I am mentally prepared to spend enough time on a target. Therefore, I am not chasing low-hanging fruits but looking for hidden gems that bug bounty programs will undoubtedly accept. It also allows me to apply what I am learning from the Web Application Hacker's Handbook and the reports I read from HackerOne's Hacktivity.

One day, I am testing a search feature of a web application. Upon sending my input, I notice that it gets reflected in the resulting page. That's a good candidate for Reflected XSS[12]. Unfortunately for me, it seems that the developer has done a great job since the output is encoded correctly. Therefore, I can't trigger any XSS.

However, while looking around and tinkering with other features, I noticed some calls to endpoints which end with the CSV[13] extension. These return inline CSV results, but there are no parameters to control. What if I try the CSV extension on the search feature? Maybe the back-end server handles both.

To my surprise, I see a prompt on my web browser page using the JavaScript payload `prompt(document.cookie)`. Hell yeah! This is what I call a real bug that I am sure will be accepted.

The next day, I am pleased to know that the program has accepted my report and rewarded me with a bounty.

The duplicate nightmare

"The person who follows the crowd will usually go no further than the crowd. The person who walks alone is likely to find himself in places no one has ever seen before." — Albert Einstein

After about a month, I finally finish reading the colossal book. I couldn't grasp all the concepts and techniques, but I have noted an exhaustive checklist I can go through whenever I need to. I can't believe how much I have learned so far! Besides, I have directly practiced some of my knowledge on real targets.

I also developed the habit of reporting only issues with a real and concrete impact, allowing me to increase my signal and reputation on HackerOne slowly. I feel that I am progressing, slowly but surely.

One night, I am hunting for bugs on one bug bounty program. I learn that the application uses AngularJS for the front-end. My reflex tells me to try Client-Side Template Injection vulnerabilities[14].

This vulnerability exploits user input that ends up in a template that the front-end technology, such as AngularJS, uses to render the page.

So I start injecting the following XSS payload `{{constructor.constructor('alert(input)')()}}` here and there while inserting the field name as input for the message. That way, if a popup triggers,

---

[14] https://portswigger.net/kb/issues/00200308_client-side-template-injection

it will show the name of the vulnerable field in the message, pretty convenient!

Suddenly, I get a popup window with the string "profile name," indicating that the payload from the profile name user input has triggered the exploit. I can hear my heart beating as I try to reproduce the issue once more. Indeed, it is vulnerable when someone visits my profile page! I quickly craft a report and send it.

The next day, the triage analyst closes it as duplicate.

When I find a valid but duplicate bug, I won't get paid, and I won't receive the full reputation points. All the fame will go to the hunter who was the first to report it.

What increases my frustration even more is that all my recent submissions have been closed as duplicates.

Just as I thought that I have finally understood the game, this duplicate nightmare has made everything much harder.

On the one hand, I have to avoid Not Applicable and Informative issues. On the other hand, I have to be the first to find a valid one. How to avoid duplicates when every decent hunter looks for known issues like XSS, CSRF, Open Redirects, and others?

Now I am starting to question the first impression I had when I first heard of bug bounty hunting from my friend. Indeed, this industry doesn't generate easy money!

If I want to avoid duplicates, I need to be the first to report a valid issue. If I want to be the first, I have to hunt for some obscure, novel, and less-known bugs. Otherwise, I need to find bugs in hidden places that most of the crowd is overlooking. The first approach requires me to learn and master more vulnerabilities, while the second approach requires me to master the art of information gathering and look for hidden places. I am leaning towards the second approach. I've learned enough vulnerabilities for now, and I need to practice.

I suddenly understand why I scored the Reflected XSS on the CSV endpoint! While the exploitation is straightforward, no one has thought of testing it because it required thinking outside the box. I believe this is one key element I should keep in mind in my future hunting. Think outside the box!

There is also another way to test for the least traveled road, and that is premium features. During my hunting, I came across web applications that have more features in paid plans. I bet a few hackers take the extra mile. Unfortunately, I am currently one of them.

Another approach would be to find new assets. So far, my focus was on the flagship web application of the bug bounty program. However, any company has many other assets, such as supporting software for accounting, HR, engineering, monitoring, and the like. There are also test environments that usually have missing security measures. Some of them might be easy to hack.

A great way to find these assets would be to discover subdomains.

I remember Jason's talk where he talked about the road less traveled. It suddenly makes sense now! I thought it was overkill, and I was wrong! It is undoubtedly a necessity.

From the videos I saw so far, there are many tools to do reconnaissance. When I started doing bug bounty hunting, the most famous ones were sublist3r[15] and

---

[15] https://github.com/aboul3la/Sublist3r

dnsdumpster[16]. Fast-forward to the future, new tools emerged, and I found myself adopting amass[17], which is now supported by the OWASP[18]. These tools use various techniques to discover subdomains, such as public data available in search engines, certificate transparency [19]logs published by Certificate Authorities, or even brute-force based on a dictionary!

Armed with amass against a top-level domain, I find many subdomains. One of them is kibana.target.com. I visit it on my web browser, but I see nothing on port 80. I google the word "kibana" to learn it is an open-source data visualization software that collects data from Elasticsearch[20] and displays it in charts and graphs. Besides, it listens on port 5601 by default. So, I append the port number to the subdomain. Here I am, looking at a dashboard filled with data about the target's internal systems! No authentication is required. Everyone is welcome!

---

[16] https://dnsdumpster.com/

[17] https://github.com/OWASP/Amass

[18] https://owasp.org/

[19] https://www.certificate-transparency.org/

[20] https://www.elastic.co/elasticsearch/service

I quickly write a report, and the program fixes it after a few hours.

This bug was a low hanging fruit waiting for anyone with decent enumeration skills to find. Yet, it was not a duplicate.

Sometimes, luck plays in your favor, and you are the first to come across it. Could that be due to a recent firewall configuration that suddenly opened the door to Kibana? I don't know. All I know is that subdomain enumeration paid-off.

I wonder how successful I would be at avoiding duplicates if I master the art of reconnaissance. That could open the door to more bugs, which will allow me to increase my reputation, improve my signal, and earn more money!

On the weekend, I meet Julia around a coffee and tell her about my progress.

— "Congratulations! You have gone a long way since we last spoke about bug bounty", she says. Then, she adds: "Now, it's time to aim for those juicy private programs."

— "Wait, private what? What's this? A secret world within bug bounty?" I astonishingly ask.

— She smiles and answers: "These are programs that you can't hack until you get an invite from HackerOne. Therefore, there is a limited number of hackers. Besides, some of them have a good scope. Do you want to know the best part? They generally tend to have higher reward amounts".

At the end of our conversation, she adds: "I am sure you will shortly receive one."

Reconnaissance and private hacks

"Time spent in reconnaissance is seldom wasted." — John Marsden

My updated strategy seems to be working like a charm. I am doing subdomain enumeration before jumping into the main web application. I am resisting the urge to file reports which would likely get closed as informative, such as user enumeration, banner grabbing, and other shallow things. Therefore, I am finding more valid bugs. Only a few of them are duplicates.

I am now aware that reconnaissance is a necessary skill for a successful bug bounty hunter. But so far, I've been doing subdomain enumeration only. If I can find more resources using other techniques, I bet it would open the door to more potential bugs.

For example, finding mergers in wide-scope programs will allow me to expand to new top-level domains, which will lead to gathering new subdomains, hence new and under-tested assets.

Another example would be gathering a list of employees. While phishing is always out-of-scope in the programs' policies, having a list of employees would still help me build a custom wordlist or prepare a list of potential accounts to use during brute-force.

A third example is looking for PDF, images, Excel spreadsheets, and Word documents. Using tools such as Foca[21], I am surprised by the kind of information stored in their metadata. In a recent security assessment in my company, a colleague collected public files about the company and gathered full names, emails, internal IP addresses, software versions, and many more.

I am looking around on the internet, trying to find any tool to help me perform broader enumeration tasks, when I come across recon-ng[22]. I learn that it is an information-gathering framework. And it looks promising! Think Metasploit[23] but for reconnaissance.

I install it on my Linux machine using the command `apt-get install recon-ng`. Then, I run it using the command `recon-ng`. Easy!

I am already familiar with Metasploit, and the look and feel are the same; I can create a workspace for each bug bounty program to keep things organized. I can enumerate subdomains, collect emails, resolve IP addresses, find people accounts on various known websites such as LinkedIn, look for any credentials

---

[21] https://www.elevenpaths.com/innovation-labs/tools/foca

[22] https://github.com/lanmaster53/recon-ng

[23] https://www.metasploit.com/

leaked in public websites, and many more! I can even generate HTML reports that contain all the findings!

Whenever I start on a new program, I run this tool and collect so much data about my target. The joy that comes from collecting such public data is so addictive that I spend too much time doing recon. Unfortunately, I lose valuable time that I'd rather spend on testing.

Indeed, too much recon is counterproductive. I need to increase my recon efficiency but avoid spending too much time, especially during the initial phase. My ideal goal would be to collect as many resources as possible in the shortest amount of time.

To achieve this, I have to automate the process and start active tests as soon as I collect an initial set of targets.

Recon-ng allows for easy automation. I can prepare a file containing all the operations I want to perform, use it as a resource with the command `recon-ng -r file` and grab a cup of coffee while the information gathering magic happens.

I can now perform quick but decent reconnaissance, with a predefined set of checks under minutes, which is a massive improvement for my bug bounty hunting methodology.

Combining reconnaissance with my web application hacking skills against public programs that pay little to no bounties allowed me to find valid bugs and increase my reputation. Then, one morning, it happens!

I receive a notification from HackerOne. When I open it, I can't believe my eyes! It is an invite to hack on a private program.

I can feel the adrenaline rush, but there is nothing better than a delicious breakfast with my family on a sunny Sunday. Bug bounty hunting can wait for an hour, or maybe two.

After spending some quality time with my family, I start hacking; I launch my recon script and perform some manual work in the meantime. After a few minutes, I have a list of subdomains, IP addresses, and contact information. Unfortunately, recon-ng doesn't find credentials this time, but I can see some emails I can test on login portals.

I then use Nmap to find alive servers and enumerate open ports on each subdomain and IP address.

I spend a few days on this program without finding anything worth reporting. Shortly after, I receive another private invite! It seems that my reputation has picked up HackerOne's interest. I gladly accept it and repeat the recon and the hacking process for the new program.

The curse of burnout

"Every great and deep difficulty bears in itself its own solution. It forces us to change our thinking in order to find it." — Neils Bohr

I have several invites now, and I am so excited that I keep jumping to new programs. Who can resist a new invite? Especially when the program has barely launched!

Unfortunately, I am violating one of my rules, which is to focus on one program, or two at most. Jumping disturbs my focus. When I lose my focus, I can't find valid bugs. As it turns out, getting into private programs has its own challenges.

Besides, I have been hacking extensively in recent months, and my routine has been tight; I would arrive home after work and immediately start hacking for hours until I am exhausted. I take about an hour for dinner, then continue hacking until midnight. Then go to bed. Wake up, go to work, come back, hunt for bugs, and repeat. I even dream of bugs!

On the weekends, I used to go out to the cinema with my friends, or travel with my family. Instead, I am recently obsessed with bug bounty hunting, and all my weekend goes on the couch, in front of the keyboard.

I have found a few valid bugs, but not enough regarding the time I have invested. Meanwhile, whenever I open my Twitter feed, I see tweets from many hunters who find bugs with generous rewards.

I am starting to feel exhausted; I don't sleep well, I don't entertain myself, rarely see my friend, and I spend less time with family. Most of my time goes between work and bug bounty hunting.

Today, I arrive home from work but can't go anywhere near my computer. I don't feel the desire to hack anymore. My self-confidence is so low that I can't even open Twitter. It is a strange feeling to hate doing something I always loved. Whenever I think of hunting for bugs, an odd negative feeling triggers immediately. I picture the amount of time I would be investing without satisfying rewards. By rewards, I mean...well, money!

Perhaps it is time to take a break for a while. With some distance, I might be able to see things clearly to solve this odd situation.

I have neglected my preparation for the OSCP since I started doing bug bounty hunting. I guess it is time to get back to it. I thought hunting for bugs would help me prepare for the certification, but I was wrong. Apart from web application hacking, there are no similarities between the two.

I focus about a month on rooting some machines from hackthebox.eu, which Julia gave me initially. Then, I purchase the three-month package and provide the OSCP course my full attention. In the first two months, I solve all the course exercises and hack the entire lab to make sure I can exploit all the vulnerabilities.

However, I notice that my approach to web hacking has changed; Most of the applications in the lab are vulnerable to known exploits. However, I am trying to enumerate the features looking for bugs like I do in the real targets. It took me some time to switch back to the CTF hacking style. Damn! Even web application hacking is different!

After rooting all the machines, I book a date for the exam.

When the day comes, I wake up, take my breakfast, and lock myself in a quiet room. It's time to hack!

Although I rooted the first two machines quickly, I am losing considerable time in the third one. It is tough as hell! It takes me the entire afternoon to finally become the administrator. I have one hour left, and I still need 5 points to pass. However, I have no lead.

Even though I took a good launch and kept myself hydrated, I couldn't stand a full day of hacking. I am so exhausted!

After 24 hours, I fail to collect enough points. Full of disappointment, I go straight to bed.

The next day, I book the retake for the next month.

All the machines are new. Luckily, I succeed this time and root all the boxes. I had to think outside the box yet keep it simple. I guess the only thing I was doing wrong in my first attempt was overthinking easy steps.

With the confidence this certification has given me, I can go back to hunting for bugs. However, I can't fall into the same mistakes once again. Indeed, taking a break has helped me put things into perspective. I think I have many problems I need to address before going any further.

The first problem is the lack of focus because of too many invitations. From now on, I won't accept all of them. Only those that satisfy my criteria will end up on my hacking list. I hope it will help me focus on a few high-quality programs.

HackerOne provides some key metrics to help me decide. The first one is the minimum bounty. I won't accept programs that offer below $100. Besides, the time to resolution should be less than a month, which has many advantages. Firstly, it will reduce the probability of duplicates because the lifetime of the bug will be shorter. Secondly, since most programs pay bounties after fixing issues, I will luckily get paid within a month. Finally, my reputation will grow fast because the team would handle my submissions quickly.

The second metric is the scope. I would prefer programs with bigger scope. This way, I guarantee to have always something interesting to work on, which will prevent boredom and keep me engaged with the program.

The third metric measures performance within the last three months. It represents the percentage of the reports that have met the program's claimed response standards. This tells me whether the program truly honors the time-to-first-response, triage, bounty, and resolution. I won't accept any program that has less than 80%.

Lastly, I will make sure that the program aligns with my values, which is one of the great things I love about bug bounty hunting; I have the freedom to choose my clients, which a typical employee generally lacks. Can you tell your boss that you won't work on a project because you don't like it? Well, I can tell it to HackerOne without risking my job.

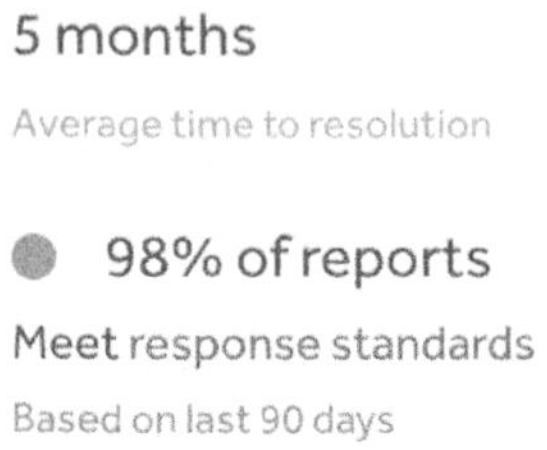

5 months
Average time to resolution

● **98% of reports**
Meet response standards
Based on last 90 days

Figure 1: Although this program meets the response standard by 98%, the time to resolution is not acceptable for me.

The second problem I face is stress. When I am stressed, I don't enjoy what I am doing. I lose focus and motivation. At least, I have to reduce it if I want to enjoy hunting for bugs.

One of the sources of stress is my Twitter feed. It is full of depressing tweets of some bug bounty hunters bragging about the money they collect from the vulnerabilities they find. I don't learn much from them because they don't contain a write-up explaining how they found those bugs. One solution would be to unfollow them all, but since some of them often tweet valuable content, I might miss a few tips.

So how am I supposed to clean my feed?

It turns out that when they find a valid bug, they usually generate a tweet directly from the bug bounty platform. On HackerOne, for example, the tweet starts with *"Yay! I was awarded"*. On Bugcrowd, it contains *"for my Submission on @Bugcrowd"*. Therefore, I can configure my Twitter feed to blacklist such expressions using the *muted words* feature.

Sweet! Now my feed is less depressing. I considerably reduced the noise!

However, even with a cleaner feed, I notice that I still get jealous when I see tweets that mention write-ups of some findings. What's wrong with me?

It turns out that whenever I see such tweets, I tend to compare myself. Since I am the losing part, I am continuously feeling low, which affects my self-confidence.

I have to switch my perspective. If someone publishes a finding, my first reaction should be gratitude, not childish jealousy! Then, I should take the time to learn something from the write-up. Maybe there is a new technique that I have never known. Or perhaps there is a new perspective I have never explored. In short, I need to be open to learning from the community continually. There is always something new to learn!

There is yet another problem related to what I have discovered so far. I focus on earning money. That explains why I get jealous of other bug bounty hunters. So far, I have read an entire heavy book, watched YouTube videos, and read blog posts about bug bounty hunting. However, I have always been aiming at money, especially when I started earning some.

What if I switched my goal from money to learning? That would eliminate all the frustration I get when I don't find bugs. At the same time, I would hack for days and still enjoy it because I do it for fun. With time, I would keep challenging my capabilities and learn new skills.

Ultimately, the money will follow. But I shouldn't hack for it. I already have a full-time job that pays my bills.

With these problems addressed, I would hopefully regain my motivation and reduce stress. However, I am sure it won't be enough. Motivation fluctuates, and I simply cannot gain momentum without consistency. Throughout this journey, I noticed that I had the most favorable results when I was working consistently. Whenever I take a significant break, my mental checklist gets weaker. In other words, I overlook some tests, and I forget some steps in my methodology, which means missing critical areas in my target.

If I want to ensure consistency, I need to set a goal and be disciplined. I don't want to focus on money because I have learned how it negatively affects my stress levels. Instead, I will focus on my reputation. What if I aim for a thousand points in six months? Would that be achievable? I grab a pencil and a piece of paper to figure that out.

I visit the reputation page on HackerOne. Each valid report gets seven points after triage. Then, depending on the severity, it gets additional points. In simple terms, a medium, high or critical severity report gets 15, 25, and 50, respectively. The average is 30 per report. I won't report low severity bugs to avoid any chance to get my submissions closed as informative. If I focus on a few programs and perform in-depth analysis, I will likely find interesting bugs. When I divide 1000 points by 37, I get around 27 reports that I should send within six months. Which means about five valid submissions per month.

That sounds realistic. However, I need to stick to it. I quickly grab my phone and write a note on my home screen that says: "5 reports per month". Doing this would help me stick to it. From experience, whenever I set a goal, I quickly forget about it in the following days. Since I grab my phone hundreds of times per day, this trick should be a good reminder.

I am still missing something

"Most of the important things in the world have been accomplished by people who have kept on trying when there seemed no hope at all." — Dale Carnegie

It is now two weeks since I set my goal, and I am not progressing a bit! Not that I don't find bugs, but I don't hack at all! Many distractions have come across my path.

One of them is travel. It's hard to work when I am supposed to spend quality time with my family. However, I am not upset. Family comes first.

The wallpaper on my phone keeps reminding me, however.

The second and biggest distraction is a side hustle job as a Security Analyst. Along with a full-time job, I can't spend what remains of my time and effort doing another cybersecurity activity.

I should have seen this coming; the side hustle job blocked my bug bounty hunting activities for a while. That is until I quit after about a year.

Strangely enough, I couldn't hack, even with the free time I have! There is something wrong with me for sure. Why does this happen to me?

For a while, I sit with myself, trying to understand the cause of my trouble, which seems to be subconscious. Shockingly, the reason was right in front of me all along. I can't hack programs I already tested!

When I think about the previous targets where I failed to find vulnerabilities, I suddenly feel a negative feeling preventing me from trying harder. I guess I am afraid of falling into the same failure again, which explains why I had kept jumping from one program to another since the beginning. Now that I have decided to focus on a few targets, my mind refuses to hack.

This is not good at all. This issue is jeopardizing my entire plan. If I continue like this, I will have to continually keep looking for new programs, which contradicts my strategy to stick to a few.

When I try to remember what I have tested in those programs, I know I have done open-source intelligence, such as subdomain enumeration, then focused on one or two assets. However, I can't remember what I did for each of them and what targets I haven't tested yet.

Could that be related to my mysterious negative feeling? I think about it for a while. Indeed, it does make sense! If I don't take notes, I lose my progress.

In fact, my mind remembers the last hunting session, which translates to a failed experience. When I want to come back the next day, or the next week, I only remember my failure! Had I documented my progress, I would have broken that feeling. A quick look into my notes would give me the next lead to follow.

I cross my fingers, hoping this would work. To test it out, I will start fresh, but only this time in order to bypass my mysterious negative feeling. For that, I need new invites, which means I must find bugs in previous programs. Or must I?

Luckily, HackerOne has just published the hacker101 educational website, where hackers can find vulnerabilities in many challenges. After accumulating enough points, they can receive private invites.

Solving some challenges would also be an excellent opportunity for me to boost my ever-low motivation and self-confidence. Plus, I will remember the old days when I enjoyed solving challenges on the root-me platform.

I solve multiple problems in one sitting, enough for me to earn a private invite. Sure enough, I receive one the next day!

Time to roll the sleeves up and focus on this new program.

Not the same mistake again

"Great losses are great lessons." —— Amit Kalantri

It is only the first week of hunting on this new program, and I have already found some bugs on the only web application in scope. It seems that the new strategy is working quite well; I am trying my best to test all the features deeply. I start from transversal security controls such as CSRF and session management, down to access control for each endpoint and injections[24] for each user input. Along the way, I don't forget to document my progress; I certainly don't want to fall into the same situation as before.

Moreover, I have access to the source code, which means I can follow a white-box approach. It is an excellent opportunity to test some of the static analysis tools and put my manual code review skills into practice. I hope I have a sharp eye to spot some bugs. Otherwise, it is never too late to learn new tricks.

Looking through the source code, I realize that it doesn't use any web application framework, which means developers must implement many security controls by hand. For example, they would need to sanitize user input, implement anti-CSRF, secure

---

[24] https://thehackerish.com/owasp-top-10-vulnerabilities-injection-explained/

SQL[25] queries, all manually. Therefore, there is a higher chance that a few hidden bugs have fallen under the cracks, waiting for me to uncover them.

I clone the code repository into my local machine and start searching for SQL queries using `grep`, a command-line tool available on Linux. For now, I am interested in SQL injections[26] because I notice a database configuration in the source code. Plus, such vulnerabilities lead to high or critical severity bugs.

My intuition was right! After about an hour, I find a user input inserted directly into a SQL query without any sanitization. Great! I found a lead. I hope I can reach the vulnerable code from the user interface.

Reading through the adjacent lines of code, I realize that the vulnerable part resides in a conditional block that is never directly reached from the user interface. That explains why I haven't been able to find it using the black-box approach.

To execute it, I have to send a GET request to a specific endpoint. Since this is a server-side bug, I can

---

[25] Structured Query Language

[26] https://thehackerish.com/sql-injection-explained-owasp-top-ten-vulnerabilities/

simply run a `curl` command or replay Burp Suite's request.

I grab Burp Suite and start playing with the endpoint. Lo and behold, I get a valid response from the server, meaning that I can reach the vulnerable code.

I tinker with the vulnerable user input until I finally trigger the vulnerability! Trying `'+or+'1'='1` gives a list of results, while `'+or+'1'='2` returns an empty list, which means this is a Blind SQL injection; I can extract data by asking the database engine a series of questions that produce true or false answers.

The next day, the program's team rates it as a high severity issue, and I get fifty reputation points because my bug is ranked higher than the average.

The following days, I get some new private invites. This time, instead of blindly accepting them, I quickly pass them through my checklist, and only one of them makes it to my hacking list. I add it to my notes and keep working on my current target. I don't want to switch to the new program until I have explored every corner of the current one.

More days come by, and my new strategy seems to have paid off. In only one web application, I have found a total of eight vulnerabilities with a severity ranging from medium to high. I am catching up on my goal, and my self-confidence is recovering.

I think it is time to move on to the new program, which seems to have a much bigger scope. It should keep me busy for a while.

Achieving my goal

"Hard work works harder than luck!" — Germany Kent

It is Saturday in the morning. I grab my laptop and start doing reconnaissance. After a brief subdomain enumeration to assess this new program's digital presence, I focus on the main web application since most of the other subdomains are an exact match. I conduct a preliminary analysis to test the waters and get a first feel of the asset's maturity.

After about ten minutes, I notice a weird 403 HTTP response, forbidding any CSRF attack against state-changing endpoints. What gets my immediate attention is the absence of any indication of anti-CSRF measures; there is no token and no validation of neither the Origin nor the Referer HTTP headers.

At this point, I have to decide if I should note it and proceed with my shallow tests or stop everything and focus on that behavior. From experience, whenever I come across strange comportment, there is a bug waiting for me to uncover. Besides, if I find something, there is a higher chance that the same bug will be everywhere in the application. That's an immense potential that I don't want to miss.

I decide to give this lead some time. If I don't find anything in the next hour, I will move on.

I tinker with every HTTP header and parameter

from the Burp Suite's CSRF proof-of-concept and replay it to understand what exactly causes my attack to fail compared to the original request. After a while, I finally find it! There is a static header missing in my PoC. To add it, I'd have to use JavaScript in an AJAX[27] call. I am not sure if I can do this. I'd have to check if I can send requests from arbitrary origins.

To my surprise, the web application allows arbitrary origins to send AJAX calls, which is a classical CORS[28] misconfiguration. I quickly alter the PoC to use JavaScript and add the missing header. Here is how it looks like.

---

[27] Asynchronous JavaScript and XML

[28] Cross-Origin Resource Sharing

```
<html>
  <body>
    <script>
      function submitRequest()
      {
        var xhr = new XMLHttpRequest();
        xhr.open("POST",
"https:\\/\\/www.redacted.com\\/api\\/resource\\/id", true);
        xhr.setRequestHeader("Accept", "application\\/json,
text\\/plain, *\\/*");
        xhr.setRequestHeader("X-Requested-With",
"XMLHttpRequest");
        xhr.withCredentials = true;
        var body = "param=value"
        var aBody = new Uint8Array(body.length);
        for (var i = 0; i < aBody.length; i++)
          aBody[i] = body.charCodeAt(i);
        xhr.send(new Blob([aBody]));
      }
    </script>
    <form action="#">
      <input type="button" value="Submit request"
onclick="submitRequest();" />
    </form>
  </body>
</html>
```

When I send it, I can't believe my eyes; the attack succeeds! I have just uncovered a bug from a simple observation of a weird behavior of the application!

I quickly file a report and cross my fingers that it is not a duplicate. Anyone with a keen eye and a decent experience can find such a bug.

I wait for about two days. Then I receive an update from the team. My heart is beating as I open the email. Oh! My report is not a duplicate! What a tremendous luck!

I open the web application to analyze the bug in-depth. After some time, I conclude that the impact matches my initial hypothesis. The bug is almost everywhere! But for some reason, I cannot reproduce it on a few features. I infer that each functionality might have its security controls against CSRF and CORS misconfigurations. Maybe each one is hosted on a separate microservice, and few of them have proper security measures against my attack.

However, what I can attack is already enough. It turns out that a simple visit to my malicious page can ruin the victim's entire account; I can manage all the victims' resources, take over their accounts, and even spread my exploit to their friends.

I file a separate report for each vulnerable feature, which results in about twenty submissions in total. After about a month, each one of them got triaged and rewarded.

Meanwhile, I kept deeply poking around the same application, which resulted in a few other vulnerabilities. I am now ahead of my scheduled plan.

Today, I open my account on HackerOne to check my last resolved report. When I have a look at my performance statistics, I can't believe my eyes! I finally crossed a thousand reputation points!

Performance stats

5.18	89th
Signal	Percentile
20.97	92nd
Impact	Percentile
1007	-
Reputation	Rank

Figure 2: Reaching 1K in reputation

I can't describe the situation! I feel a satisfying sense of accomplishment, but I am staring at the screen in disbelief. Meanwhile, I keep repeating to myself: I finally achieved my goal!

The end?

"Every new beginning comes from some other beginning's end."
— Jenna Evans Welch

Throughout this fascinating journey, I learned so many things.

Firstly, bug bounty hunting is not easy. It is a challenging marathon that you should take seriously as any other job. If you don't enjoy constant learning or get afraid of being challenged all the time, you should look for something else.

Secondly, hunting for bugs in real targets is different from hacking in CTFs; While challenges taught me how to exploit individual vulnerabilities, bug bounty hunting requires broader technical expertise. I learned that focus, reconnaissance, and in-depth testing are vital ingredients for reducing duplicate and informative submissions.

Thirdly, bug bounty hunting taught me how to adapt; I learned how to shift my mindset from looking for money to harvesting knowledge. Besides, I learned how taking organized notes, setting achievable goals, being consistent, and having discipline is as crucial as technical knowledge. I can confidently confirm that these soft skills make the difference between an amateur and a professional bug bounty hunter.

Finally, bug bounty hunting allowed me to discover more of my flaws, push the limits of my capabilities, and be a better version of myself.

Now it's time to celebrate my achievement with my family, then think of my next goal.

Appendix A: Approach a new target

This checklist contains explained steps to get you started quickly when you first engage with a bug bounty program.

Don't forget to change the keyword **DOMAIN** to match your target's domain name throughout this checklist.

1. OSINT

Open-source intelligence is the process of gathering publicly available data about your target, such as subdomains, contact information, exposed files and credentials, etc.

There are a lot of sources to use when you enumerate. Here is a list of useful ones, but feel free to explore other tools on your own. The best way to learn reconnaissance it to practice with as many tools and techniques as possible, then adopt the ones that suit your preferences and taste. For example, if you like to use the terminal, you will naturally prefer command-line tools.

1.1. Google Dorking

Uses Google operators to find interesting bits of information about your target. Some examples are:

Google dork	Description

`site:sub.DOMAIN`
`site:.*.DOMAIN`
`site:.*.*.DOMAIN`
	Gives you only the pages under a specific domain or subdomain using the `site` operator.
	
	You can also enumerate subdomains using wildcards. You can even find subdomains in deeper levels using asterisks.

`site:DOMAIN AND (ext:xslx OR docx OR pdf)`	You can combine multiple operators. For example, on the left is a query to find all indexed PDF, Excel and Word

	documents hosted on **DOMAIN**.
The Google Hacking Database (https://www.exploit-db.com/google-hacking-database)	This is the database of Google dorks. You can search by keyword or category. For example, if you have found that the target uses Java, search on the database and you'll find results such as `intext:jdbc:oracle filetype:java`, which returns all Java files that are known to contain passwords.

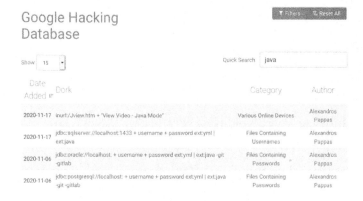

Figure 3: Google Hacking Database results for the keyword "java"

1.2. File metadata

Foca is a great tool for analyzing meta-data inside the files of your target. Say you have found many PDF files using your previous Google dorking technique, you can leverage Foca to extract meta-data from these documents, like the author, the location, the software being used, the date of the creation, sensitive data, etc.

This data is valuable when you want to understand more on the technologies and the users of your target. Foca can also accept a domain as input and searches Google, Bing and DuckDuckGo for indexed files, then performs meta-data extraction and analysis.

The downside is that it works on Windows only, so you may want to use a virtual machine or a dual boot if you don't have Windows as a primary OS.

1.3. Enumeration using theharvester

TheHarvester[29] allows you to gather a list of emails, subdomains, IPs and URLs from public sources for a particular domain. It is present on Kali Linux, but you can easily download it on other Linux distributions. To install it using Docker, run:

```
git clone
https://github.com/laramies/theHarvester
cd theHarvester

docker build -t theharvester .
```

You can use it as follows to gather data from all sources:

```
docker run theharvester -b all -d DOMAIN
```

---

[29] https://github.com/laramies/theHarvester

1.4. DNS Enumeration

DNS enumeration allows you to understand where your target is located and what third-party services it uses. If there are any misconfiguration, you might even take over a subdomain or perform DNS zone transfers[30].

To grab data about the target's DNS, you can use either Dig. Run the following commands:

```
sudo apt update
sudo apt install dnsutils
dig ANY DOMAIN
```

Additionally, you can use fierce to do in-depth DNS enumeration and automate checks for neighbor IP addresses and zone transfer attacks. Learn how to use all its capabilities using the GitHub page[31].

```
sudo apt update
sudo apt install python3 python3-pip
python3 -m pip install fierce
```

---

[30] https://en.wikipedia.org/wiki/DNS_zone_transfer

[31] https://github.com/mschwager/fierce

1.5. Subdomains enumeration

Enumerating subdomains is a crucial step in your enumeration phase. It allows you to gather a list of potential assets and understand the naming convention. Since many targets use the same public domain for internal services, you can also enumerate internal hosts. Then, look for ways to reach them, such as abusing a VPN entry.

There are many techniques to enumerate subdomains.

1.5.1. Certificate transparency using Crtsh

Go to `https://crt.sh`. Then, input `%.DOMAIN` to get a list of subdomains. You can use this one-liner to automate the process, inspired by snwlol's script[32].

```
curl -k -s https://crt.sh/?q=%.$1 | grep $1 |
grep TD | sed -e 's/<//g' | sed -e 's/>//g' |
sed -e 's/BR/\n/g' | sed -e 's/TD//g' | sed -
e 's/\\/\//g' | sed -e 's/ //g' | sed -n
'1!p' | cut -d"/" -f1 | sort -u
```

---

[32] https://github.com/snwlol/crt.sh/blob/master/crt.sh

Make it executable and run it.

```
chmod 755 oneliner.sh
./oneliner.sh DOMAIN
```

1.5.2. Amass

This is the reference tool for subdomain enumeration so far. It is now part of the OWASP projects.

I prefer to use the Docker version.

The installation steps can be found[33] on Github. The user manual[34] contains all what you need to get started.

Once you install it, the most basic command for subdomain enumeration is:

```
amass enum -d DOMAIN
```

---

[33] https://github.com/OWASP/Amass/blob/master/doc/install.md

[34]

https://github.com/OWASP/Amass/blob/master/doc/user_guide.m
d

1.5.3. Brute-forcing subdomains

You can use amass with the –brute option like this:

amass enum –brute –d DOMAIN

You can also use altdns to generate a list of potential subdomains, and massdns find valid ones using brute-force.

Run the following commands to set them up:

```
pip3 install py-altdns

git clone
https://github.com/blechschmidt/massdns.
git

cd massdns
make
sudo ln -s /usr/local/bin/massdns
bin/massdns
```

You can then use the following workflow to get a greppable JSON file that you can parse afterward.

```
altdns -i subdomains_input.txt -o
output.txt -w wordlist

massdns -r resolvers.txt -t A
potential_subdomains.txt -w output -o J
```

Note: The best talk, in my humble opinion, about subdomain brute-forcing is Frans Rosen's[35], it covers not only brute-forcing, but also how to test for NXDOMAIN, SERVFAIL and REFUSED DNS responses, plus a bit more. I highly recommend it.

By now, you will have subdomains, emails and hopefully juicy files and credentials. It's time to find the running services.

2. Probe live assets

In this step, you will filter subdomains and IP addresses that have some running services that you can hack.

2.1. Nmap

Run the following command to find live servers. `subdomains.txt` file contains the list of potential subdomains you gathered from the previous steps.

```
nmap -sn -iL subdomains.txt
```

---

[35] https://www.YouTube.com/watch?v=HhJv8CU-RIk

2.2. Httprobe

You can use Tomnomnom's httprobe[36] tool if you are just interested in web applications. Run this command:

```
cat subdomains.txt | httprobe | tee
webapps.txt
```

You will get a list of HTTP and HTTPS assets that you can start hacking.

Note: You can use custom port numbers. Read the documentation of the tool on the GitHub page.

2.3. Screenshot the web applications

When the number of subdomains is significant, it is not practical to manually visit every web application. I use aquatone[37] to quickly spot interestingly looking assets.

---

[36] https://github.com/tomnomnom/httprobe

[37] https://github.com/michenriksen/aquatone#installation

In the following command, aquatone will probe web assets based on a large sample of potential ports and output the results into the specified folder.

```
cat subdomains.txt | aquatone -ports
large -out ~/aquatone/DOMAIN
```

3. Port scanning

The scanning in the early phases of enumeration doesn't help much. It takes time and generates a lot of traffic for low returns. Therefore, it won't take a big portion of this guide.

Note: You can use the search engine shodan.io to get a list of open ports without performing port scanning.

3.1. Fast Nmap TCP and UDP scans

To find running services on the twenty most famous TCP ports, run:

```
nmap --top-ports 20 -iL subdomains.txt
```

To find open UDP ports for known services, such as SNMP, POP, TFTP, run:

```
nmap -sU -p990,110,69,161 -iL subdomains.txt
```

3.2. Masscan

Useful for a large number of IP addresses, but be careful; It generates a lot of traffic on your target. Don't do it unless the client allows you.

To use masscan, you first need to resolve the subdomains list you found. Use the following one-liner:

```
cat subdomains.txt | xargs -n1 host |
grep "has address" | cut -d" " -f4 | sort
-u > ips.txt
```

Then, use masscan to scan all ports:

```
masscan -p0-65535 -iL ips.txt --rate 100000
```

By now, you will have an exhaustive list of web applications. The next appendix will guide you through the web application hacking process.

Appendix B: Web hacking checklist

This is a list of checks you can perform against web applications. It focuses on enumeration and web application testing.

Note that you have to change the **SERVER** keyword to your target server.

1. Scan the running services

Before focusing on the main web application present on the subdomain or IP address, it is always a good idea to enumerate other potential services running on the same server. You might find other under-tested web applications.

To scan all TCP ports of the web app and output the results into xml, greppable and Nmap formats, use this command.

```
nmap -p- -oA output SERVER
```

2. Directory enumeration

Once you find a web application, you can perform directory brute-forcing using Nmap, run:

```
nmap --script=http-enum TARGET -pPORT
```

You can also use Wfuzz with the top disallowed robots' wordlist from the SecLists Github project[38].

Run the following command to install and run Wfuzz. Note that you should keep the keyword **FUZZ**. Wfuzz uses it to know where to fuzz.

```
sudo apt install wfuzz

wfuzz -z
file,/path/to/seclists/Discovery/Web_Cont
ent/Top1000-RobotsDisallowed.txt
SERVER/FUZZ
```

3. JavaScript enumeration

JavaScript files are a treasure trove for any bug bounty hunter, especially if the application uses a front-end technology, such as AngularJS or React.

---

[38] https://github.com/danielmiessler/SecLists

You can find sensitive comments, passwords, endpoints and other data.

LinkFinder is a tool that allows you to extract links from JavaScript files.

Run the following commands to setup LinkFinder.

```
git clone
https://github.com/GerbenJavado/LinkFind
er.git

cd LinkFinder
sudo python3 setup.py install
pip3 install -r requirements.txt
```

Then, use it with the command:

```
python3 linkfinder.py -i WEB_PAGE|JS_LIST -o result.html
```

The tool will parse the HTML page, or a file containing a list of JavaScript files and give you the HTML output results.

You can paste the following JQuery code inside your web browser's console to extract the list of URLs from the HTML report.

```
$$("span[style='background-
color:yellow']").forEach(function(e){con
sole.log(e.innerHTML);});
```

One way to use them would be to copy-paste the list into Burp Suite's Intruder and see if you hit a new resource.

4. Parameter discovery

Parameth is a tool that allows you to brute-force parameter names, which helps you to discover hidden features. You can also use Burp Suite's Param Miner extension[39].

Run the following commands to install and use Parameth. More options can be found on the GitHub page[40].

```
git clone https://github.com/maK-
/parameth.git

cd parameth
pip install -r requirements.txt

python parameth.py -u http://SERVER/URL
```

[39] https://www.YouTube.com/watch?v=IYk7-xvOMOo

[40] https://github.com/maK-/parameth

5. Enumerate the web app technologies

Understanding the web application technologies helps you tailor your tests, focus on key vulnerabilities, and search for specific files using Google dorks. I like to use Wappalyzer, which fingerprints the technologies being used by the application whenever you visit a web page.

To use Wappalyzer, install the extension on your favorite web browser. A new icon will appear in the top-right corner. When you visit a web page, you can click on it and learn what this application is using.

Figure 4: HackerOne uses Ruby on Rails and React

If any known software/framework is used, use tools like searchsploit[41] to discover known vulnerabilities and their public exploits.

By now, you should have a list of technologies, endpoints, files with potentially sensitive data.

If you are lucky, you have usernames, passwords and exploits for outdated technologies. You can use them to directly exploit the web application. Otherwise, it's time to roll up your sleeves and test the application directly using a web browser and a web proxy, like Burp Suite[42] or ZAProxy[43].

6. Analyzing the web application

There is no magic here. You simply use the application as intended while proxying the traffic through Burp Suite or ZAP. If the application is small, run Burp or ZAP spider while excluding any out-of-scope resources to cover most of your target.

---

[41] https://www.exploit-db.com/searchsploit

[42] https://thehackerish.com/owasp-top-10-training-for-burp-suite/

[43] https://thehackerish.com/owasp-top-10-training-setup-for-owasp-zap/

When browsing and analyzing your application, always try to understand the bigger picture. Some of the things you can check are as follows.

6.1. Entry points

Enumerating all the entry points allows you to maximize your chances of finding bugs.

Look how the application communicates with your browser. For example, modern web application use APIs. Therefore, you can look if it follows a RESTful convention. If it is the case, try possible injections inside the URL. For example, if you have an endpoint such as `/api/accounts/name`, you can try `/api/accounts/'+or+1=1+--+` for a SQL injection.

Make a note of GET and POST parameters and look for any interesting ones. For example, a filter parameter in a search feature is likely to be used in a SQL query inside the `where` clause.

Tinker with HTTP headers, such as the Referer, User-Agent, Host and X-Forwarded-For, and look how the application responds. If it returns different output, you might be traversing a reverse proxy along the way. Here is an example[44] of how you can abuse the Host header.

Locate session tokens and understand what type is used, how the application generates, stores, and transmits them. For example, the application might use JWT tokens[45], or session cookies.

Enumerate all the features of the application, including the premium ones.

Notice any divergence from the standard user interface, parameter names, endpoint convention, etc. There might be a lack of proper security compared to the rest of the application.

6.2.   Mapping the attack surface

The following table lists potential vulnerabilities that you usually exist on the behavior you spot when browsing each feature. Use it as a source of inspiration when you want to find an attack angle.

Note: You have to prove a concrete impact before

---

[44] https://youtu.be/MQCJJXH4db8

[45] https://youtu.be/SuDN35-aefY

sending your report to a bug bounty program, otherwise it will likely be closed as informative, at best.

Behavior	Potential vulnerabilities
Identifiable web server	Common misconfiguration, known exploits.
Third-party components	Known vulnerabilities and public exploits.
Email interaction	Email/command injection.
Error messages	Information disclosure.
Off-site links	Leakage of query strings in the Referer.
User impersonation	Privilege escalation, account takeover.
Access Control	Horizontal and vertical escalation.
Session tokens	Predictable tokens, insecure generation or handling of session tokens.

Multistage functions	Logic flaws.
Login	Username enumeration, weak passwords, brute-force.
Dynamic redirects	Redirection and header injection.
Reflected input	HTML injection, XSS.
File upload/download	RCE, XXE, Path traversal.
Database interaction	SQL/NoSQL injection.
Client-side validation	Checks may not be replicated on the server.

Organize the finding by building a functional map diagram that lists functions with their inputs and outputs.

Based on the result of your analysis, formulate a plan of attack, prioritizing the most interesting-looking functionality and the most serious of the associated potential vulnerabilities.

6.3. Additional testing tips

Navigate the application with JavaScript enabled and disabled, same thing for cookies. You might detect a weird behavior when you hit a use case that the developers didn't anticipate.

To disable JavaScript in Firefox, go to the address bar and type `about:config` and set the key `javascript.enabled` to `false`. To disable cookies, got to settings > Privacy > history > don't accept cookies.

To find hidden content, here are some instructions.

— Notice keywords like "test this function" and "TODO" comments in the JavaScript code or the HTML comments. They might reveal hidden endpoints or incomplete features.

— Send manual requests to known valid and invalid resources and note how the server handles it. Then, use a wordlist with Wfuzz or ffuf[46] to enumerate directories.

---

[46] https://github.com/ffuf/ffuf

— Use Burp Suite's Intruder tool with custom endpoints based on the patterns you learned. For example, if a feature uses the endpoint /getThat, try /deleteThis, /removeThat, /addThat, etc).

— Use the Intruder to brute-force resources identified by integers. For example, if there is and endpoint of the form /accounts/10, try /accounts/11. You might access unauthorized accounts.

— Review JavaScript, HTML and CSS code, and look for banners, Ajax requests, form actions and comments for any additional endpoints.

— Reuse Wfuzz, this time including the newly found resources, and add extensions such as: txt, bak, src, inc, old, java and cs, etc. to download any static files which contain server-side code.

Printed in Great Britain
by Amazon